Objects of Hunger

CRAB ORCHARD SERIES IN POETRY

FIRST BOOK AWARD

Objects of Hunger

POEMS BY E.C. BELLI

Crab Orchard Review & Southern Illinois University Press

CARBONDALE

Southern Illinois University Press
www.siupress.com

22 21 20 19   4 3 2 1

Cover illustration: "The Land Knows," by Bridgette Guerzon Mills

The Crab Orchard Series in Poetry is a joint publishing venture of
Southern Illinois University Press and *Crab Orchard Review*. This
series has been made possible by the generous support of the Office
of the President of Southern Illinois University and the Office of the
Vice Chancellor for Academic Affairs and Provost at Southern Illinois
University Carbondale.

Editor of the Crab Orchard Series in Poetry: Jon Tribble
Judge for the 2018 First Book Award: Chad Davidson

Library of Congress Cataloging-in-Publication Data
Names: Belli, E. C., author.
Title: Objects of hunger / E. C. Belli.
Description: Carbondale : Southern Illinois University Press, 2019. |
    Series: Crab Orchard series in poetry
Identifiers: LCCN 2018026745 | ISBN 9780809337255 (paperback) |
    ISBN 9780809337262 (ebook)
Subjects: | BISAC: POETRY / American / General.
Classification: LCC PS3602.E6477 A6 2019 | DDC 811/.6—dc23 LC
    record available at https://lccn.loc.gov/2018026745

CONTENTS

I. WHAT WAS

Argument 3

Junipers 4

The Road 5

The Pepper Shakers Were Filled to the Brim with Hosts
of Swallows 6

Visual Analysis of Grief and You 7

Death Toll 8

II. A MONTH OF GRIEVANCES

Negotiation 11

Expectations 12

Afternoon 13

Disagreement 14

Concerns 15

Dispatch 16

The Unmentionable Worship of Idle Afternoons 17

Resolution 18

Opposition 19

Devotion 20

Optimism 21

Revelation 22

Nonchalance 23

Apology 24

Politics 25

Opinions 26

Persistence 27

Intimate 28

Couples Going Nude into the Sad Water 29

Wonderment 30

Littoral 31

Acrimony 32

All the Arts of Hurting 33

Proposal 34

The Immortelles of Perfect Pitch 35

Seduction Act 36

Parameters 37

Mercy 38

Beginnings 39

Saturnine 40

III. BLUR

What Was Said 43

Tête-à-Tête 44

The Possibility of an Ending 45

Almost a Lament 46

Postpartum 47

The Question of Surrender 48

An Autobiography of Asphalt 49

Memory 50

IV. MIGHT

Winding Down 53

One Dog Will Find Us Both 54

Sentience (cont'd) 55

Swallows 56

Vigilance 57

The Then & Now of Dusks 58

The Letter 59

Substance 60

The Only Love Poem 61

Manifest 62

Migrations 63

Notes 65

Acknowledgments 73

If there is justice in some other world, those
like myself, whom nature forces
into lives of abstinence, should get
the lion's share of all things, all
objects of hunger, greed being
praise of you.
> —"Vespers [Once I believed in
> you . . .]" by Louise Glück

You, true mortar.
> —"Still?" by Wassily Kandinsky
> (trans. Elizabeth R. Napier)

Objects of Hunger

1. *What Was*

ARGUMENT

Snow in both our dreams—what
does this mean? Some sort
of presage, I
imagine, but
I was never too
prescient
Always too present
Go, you
say, and I do
hardly bitter
merely protracted
like some kind
of cool
collected snow

JUNIPERS

The snow
Like a foreword
Perhaps the light is made of angels
Perhaps they do not break
Don't think that because they were made
By men
They won't come apart
Most things men want
Come apart
(Like my legs)
You smile
Then I say
The light isn't made of angels, you fool
It's made of heartbreak

THE ROAD

Do you remember
taking that hard
left into the night
How we were—
primeval & bare
Two blurs
sparring
in a prolonged clamor
by the water
On good nights, I remember
it all, down
to the burrs
On bad days,
only by the way
the fish
were biting the stars

THE PEPPER SHAKERS WERE FILLED TO THE BRIM WITH HOSTS OF SWALLOWS

They were very hard to close
The colossal sun in the rearview was a heartthrob
Dogs barking in the nighttime were torrid memories of the moon
And the people were all just wonderful
But something sat in the blood
Aged poorly
Left us like old skies
There was a gray hair
And then there was another

VISUAL ANALYSIS OF GRIEF AND YOU

GRIEF: holy—unapologetic—budding
YOU: coming on tender, but a terror
GRIEF: terminal—alluring—nocturnal
YOU: so utterly consumptive like blue
GRIEF: resolute—blind—kind
YOU: fire, sometimes biting in the brittle
GRIEF: vast—infinitesimal—biting
YOU: mauve of dawn, always
GRIEF: like frost—like fire—like fumes
YOU: ready to leave, nocturnal and immensely
GRIEF: absolute—efflorescent—tender
YOU: unapologetic, of course

DEATH TOLL

It was never just a tremor
that night
       like a field on fire
and it was never
a question
of who returns
the love
       to you
love is always
a victim and an accused
why see it in such bold colors
why can't there
just be
two victims
the way
it actually is
       simple as
one   two

11. *A Month of Grievances*

NEGOTIATION

Nobody has time for grief—
He says, Look at the bird,
Not because
He actually cares
About the bird
But because he cares about you
Caring about him
Caring about the bird—
Do you see
How it goes?
Now, he says, each placental
Has its marsupial equivalent
Apart, they evolved
Into the same exact things—
They are a negative
Of us, who, together,
Evolved into opposite poles
You, resin to my pollen
You, air to my roots

EXPECTATIONS

Dawn unbridled across the plain, and dream
Severed from the body, at last
A foot in front
Of the other—
The thing you call life
By which you mean
Weeping controllably
In the amount of one tablespoon
A day (approx.)
By which you mean
Bravura and colloidal oatmeal cream
After breakfast
You see, if you'll just follow
The recipe
It will all go *singingly*

AFTERNOON

the ridge
in the wild sun
through smoke and wire
roaring with shovels
and bristling gray
it grapples in our eyes
we flounder
on the water
like old suns

DISAGREEMENT

Whose voice makes an emptiness of night—
Moon, at the brim of song
The woodlands sit baffled, exhausted
Like my malfunctioning body under no hand
There are storms at my helm
And nothing for proof of my love
I call it a lure
The way the light crowds the mountaintops
You call it a plight
How the mountains here aren't really mountains
At all

CONCERNS

Rain sharp, darkening
All lion and no desire
You were held almost true
Like love with disaster written in its place
I've always liked that word—*scarlet*
It has such bright hair
Are you afraid to fight, I ask
Are you, you say—
Only of the night

DISPATCH

Now, here's a blunder
Complete with wings and a solid frame
It's bad to think of control:
It drives the jabber out of the trees
Later, some relief—the dripping
Obscurity and its hanging head
I stand quiet as shelves
Next to your wisdom of nails
And your silence that bumps and flutters
Like a crowd of June bugs in their copper armors
We're all a bit breathless these days, I'd say
Especially the men, all worn out
With self-pity
It's all quiet
Guns and mean whispers
On this front, I'd say
Just another day

THE UNMENTIONABLE WORSHIP OF IDLE AFTERNOONS

Shadows of June
outspread in you—
and the larks flew off
(I hear ramparts seem more still up close)
Sweet grass
watched you go
Then there was word of distant fights,
talk of mourning
those terrible mothers—
the ones screaming by the fire,
treading on your face
Who says dreams end
None of this ever ends

RESOLUTION

How are things found
with eyes shut—
Remark the brain
patrolling in the dark,
crawling with hopeless give
And all that fighting
tonight is a blank ache
What wounds aren't worthwhile?
Can you stay awake
a moment longer, please
I'd like to speak
about those men
you keep out back
Can't you see they've been out too long—
They're all blind with stars
No, you say,
They never had eyes
in the first place
I know it, you say,
Because they never
wanted to touch
my face

OPPOSITION

the peaceful bed
the work of light
upon clay, a hollow
storm in an away
I glare unholy
at the faces and forms
then your nape—
head secure:
what glorious end to your
spine!
I wonder where struggle
lives in you—
I'd like to say the loins
But you're not that kind of man
You're one
for tired looks
for the crushing weight of
intellect
for what usurps
all the little
blessings

DEVOTION

All those lonely, saintless wars:
Unlike its name, gloom is quiet.
It is a savage thing, a face
How we wear our eyes like wounds
I have found that stairs
are a much friendlier place
than you'd give them credit for.
Not at all like life—a twilight
space without creatures or surges
or hair. Just two simple choices.
Up or down. The simplicity
of flight: it would blow your mind.

OPTIMISM

Rust morning. Again,
the incompetent heart speaks
the language of stones.
I tell you, in the voice
of the old poet: move it
into the sun. It will warm.
Like the fields and their seeds,
the clay and beams.
Happiness is a riot of endless
limbs. You say, Hope
is the light at the end—
I say, It is what keeps us
drenched and dredging
through this darkness
for one day more.

REVELATION

I escaped the dull granite
and reached your face by hunting
some kind of wilderness.
What a strange playing field it is—
leaving your opponent undone,
hopeless like that. It's glee we need
to temper all this truth-telling.
Perhaps lies are the better way.
Perhaps lies aren't really as bad as they are
made out to be. I think honesty
is just a different word for carnage.

NONCHALANCE

We're like retreating citadels, you say,
Now turn off the lamp.
Darkness isn't an outside thing—
it lives somewhere in the forehead:
like some special kind of ache.
Dawn sags forever on the horizon;
I am all wires and brambles
but I am here—even with eyes
crusted with night. Think of all
the promise a new day entails.

APOLOGY

Another battering, brown grass.
Sundown is a musing ruin,
a tired gaze. Do you know it
by any other name?
I am supremely content
though I despise board games
and Sunday afternoons.
Put on a decent face, I'd like to say
some days. We're all crushed
with longing. Last week,
I left the dog with someone
who almost let him die. It didn't matter
to her—his trench-deep eyes,
four sturdy legs, a trodden heart
endless with hope (all the
little things that make you
you). One person in the world
loved him, you see—made him
less wretched, which is to say
easier to maim without remorse.
Love is always a good cause
for injury.

POLITICS

Clouds shift, return
holier still. *Radiance*
is whispered like a name.
All those people talking with faces
like hearses have never been
more heartless. How awkward and still—
the luminous days in houses
resplendent with complicity (and ours
has rarely been more strained, though
happiness is imminent. I await it
like an epiphany). I always broke things
in people's houses, left hollows
where there were once things.
My sweet wreckage
abandoned
in a troubled blue, and a
hush. By luck,
there were other children
to blame. I let them have it,
those gleeful fools—you might call it
some form of
redistribution. Perhaps I am
a socialist
at heart.

Solemnities of stillness
and noon
ripens under our feet.
Would you call this crush
of land copper or bronze—
you were never very good
with colors after all.
I first noticed
when I was still
blind. Now,
all your little distortions
are just more flesh.

PERSISTENCE

What grieves—
years wild with hopelessness,
hours untold
I prefer beauty when it is
spoiled because then the
men don't come by
We trade in pity:
you are sorry
I am still weeping
over the same
tired things (even oil
spills get old), and you
are a sanctuary
of want
I love the new lines
on my forehead—they mean
I am still here
Won't you slip
your steady eyes
through my running hair
just this once

INTIMATE

The past still hunched in a corner
Like someone's uncle
Spring moves in with its muffled gloom
I despise the smell of a fire going
Out, and the door
Yawning another sunlit crowd through—
To build days out of blight
While somebody sings:
That is what the future holds
But I love being alone—I don't need people
To love, you say
It's all marveling until they come alive,
You say
Then you called me *September*, waiting
While others slipped through doors
Saying words like *brain   guilt   heroes*

COUPLES GOING NUDE INTO THE SAD WATER

after Lawrence Ferlinghetti

What is revealed in their quiet conferences—
That the dignity of water calls for whispers
Or that winter is for fights, absolution, not aquatic
Life. Remembrance lies savage
With regret. Years will always outshine skill,
Come what may. Out of the conversations
Our faces built, guilt was passed over twice.
It's not that we *can't* talk about it—
It's just that our bodies keep getting in the way.

WONDERMENT

Knowing our marveling has come
To a close
We hang like glass
Pondering the field, the sorrowing
Trees, men
Unstirred
Words like flares—use them right
And they could save us
From anything
Why must tenderness engender
Such alarm?
It's no worse than the sun
On tin cups
A change of course would be
So easy, were it not
For the lure
Of inhumanities:
Silence, thought

LITTORAL

Waiting for boys got old, like a tired
hymn. You're lovelier than the gathering
day, than all my pretty sleep, than glowing
towns. I want to hold you like the terror
of illness. Call you artist. Call you solemn.
Mostly it's your waist that lures me.
I love you sorrowful, and when you speak.
How badly we were both held—
Together we could be our own institute,
Find crowds of recruits who know about
Lapsed care, things that burn inside even
When you are sitting, or awake.
Do you need bandages, company—
What can I do. Above all, I remember
your arms. Why won't you call—

ACRIMONY

old dreams are robins
setting off
for hours
a faint mourning
and then russet
we confer
while the guests
sit like flaws
they keep returning
despite our best efforts
mothers are holy
but more often
they are laced with
a special brand
of obscurity
we call memories

Brute eyes worn like medals.
He's all arms, and three parts hell.
With nothing more to spare.
I've got no years more glorious,
no creed to compare: my being
merely limited to bringing about
life. They must have lovers—
those men sturdy as bridges—
who know what it is to sweep
at night, to catch the boys hitting,
to be merry willingly. Springward
seems an impossibility for most of us
now. But as long as there are
lungs, there will be rot. Slow days
have their joys. Perhaps
a good first step would be to watch
the flowers. How even dust
accumulating on a leaf can kill them.
How to injure, but not maul.
You see, I haven't taken out the duster
in months: I'm as cold-blooded as you.

PROPOSAL

Down the darkening way,
lined lamps
guard our front—I wouldn't
call it a war;
there are still birds, pale
flowers, the scent
of a woman.
I always thought
rainloads
of silence and wild
melancholy
were the recipe
for *old* love—
(perhaps
I must learn to
listen better,
perhaps I lack
inquisitiveness
as you always say
—aren't I bitter,
and you a seer).
Instead,
I found
those are the steps
to be taken
in order
to make love
disappear.
Are you free?
Let's go now.
Put on your shoes.
I love making love
crumble
with you.

THE IMMORTELLES OF PERFECT PITCH

after Seamus Heaney

It's a slow shuffle this morning,
the house orchestral
in its awakening.
Bare your palms now—
what batter
of appeals expect me
at the door?
We're all fumbling
along, you know,
no matter how keen.
I'll keep wandering,
to avoid your
tongue. Wading ravished
gives me life.
Can't we trade words
instead of clarion calls,
just this once?
But I want to use big words
to define your deeds—
carnage,
shattered—out of hope
you might hear them,
I suppose. I don't know
what I was thinking.
I'm already back
to default. Tongue-tied.

SEDUCTION ACT

Rye heaves
as the men
leave the field.
They're so close, the gray
undaunted
by their footsteps.
Moon glares;
Honey, don't look
so forlorn, they blare
like barbarians again.
Poor muse,
so naked
in her flesh of
phosphorus,
so public,
so eternally
consumed.

PARAMETERS

Despondency gets old
and when the heart goes
unanswered, we're awfully prone
to monstrosity. Why not
singing, I wonder,
the more natural order
for raising the spirit?
Isn't it saddening
to watch ourselves receding,
resigned, provoked
like that. You, me:
two giant mouths.

MERCY

The books won't speak
about dominion
or pity—elegies for the sun
fill their bounds.
What else is consolatory?
Generations of hot days
threatening to last
forever. I remember
going home,
letting their names
out into the fields.

BEGINNINGS

Think of all the sadness
the word *weaning* entails—
sap traded for grain,
need wiped away
as though by soft
invisible rains—
the small plant uprooted
from its meadow. Home
is flesh first, a place
second, memory
last—that's where
we stopped,
as though caught
midthroat.
Your touch crashes
against my skin again.
What comforts are still
available—I can't even
use soap. I imagine
there will come a day
soon
when I will feel
fresher, live
for a while
outside the confines
of what is useful,
without these terribly
common wounds.

SATURNINE

We're immune to the stars now—
here on the shores of reciprocity.
Heart placid, the arithmetic of simple
tasks running through the veins.
There is a dullness nothing solves—
vital days withering into dusks
so forlorn I barely know them.
I never knew myself this taciturn;
troops of stillness filling me to the
brim. I dream ache will swoop in,
and, like cautery, move my feet,
jolt the sores, remind me to sing.

III. *Blur*

WHAT WAS SAID

Fleshless battalions go—the night patrol
Heaped mass of
Words with one face
Tripping over wires
Small scalding coils
In the little church
Of your mouth—
Goodbye,
Or sparrows

TÊTE-À-TÊTE

tight hours & pity sunrises
the furniture/ferns collecting
our breathless topics:
how fast the trees
are ending in tuning forks
& the birds are mistakes
in a hard sun
you know, we're nothing more
than flesh under the eaves

THE POSSIBILITY OF AN ENDING

On the borders of tender
How it all blurs—
Under bold towers of foliage
We are such wet and sad machines
My feet are short sentences
The cat, a paragraph
Her coiled weight on my chest
Locust eyes
Small signs of the apocalypse

ALMOST A LAMENT

Your eyes are a forge—
I've only ever known you scalding
Your thick neck, so ancient
And a glory
I love the thought that
You could break me
Or that you don't—
That somehow I'm worth
Remaining
And when you talk to me
Like an air, a pavane
Raining remarkable words
Down my face, into
My little brick and mortar ears—
The tremendous thought
That those words are mine
Tell me why I deserve them

POSTPARTUM

Sometimes I'm full of dread—
Like the edge of nations
It's a slow rot
The kind that whispers
And divides you
As though you were
Truly yarn
Anything sets off
The pangs
Lately it has been
The mention
Of wandering
And then that song—
The one where
The little cat
Licks the cheese
At the end

THE QUESTION OF SURRENDER

Senseless passersby
Like dull mackerels
The sun elegiac
The day seemed to come
With apologies
I'm sorry too,
I say—
For *being*
Some experiences
Like living
Are so laced
With guilt
Where was
The night
In all this?

AN AUTOBIOGRAPHY OF ASPHALT

Night came down like gauze
then the mechanical requests
& lavender desires
Blouses like blossoms against the erotic fruit
inside closed spaces
Then suddenly something
like hope: the resolute frost
clinging to the lonesome
pavement, its brutal longings—
Pavements make me sad, don't you know
I haven't seen them in so long

MEMORY

This divine hour
is for torn things:
the light, the soles
of my feet, the
sheets between
my legs.

IV. *Might*

WINDING DOWN

It smells like snow—
How visible
the petulant flow
raining down
its soft dissent
I see us everywhere: the majestic
shadows, the petty rivalry
of churches
piercing through like flint
or is it
in the gentle concussions
of voices
bouncing off the eaves
at a little past midnight
something foaming at the mouth
like wild dogs
in such strange and sad raptures
Only a milk-thin pastoral
will ever remember
this

ONE DOG WILL FIND US BOTH

after Djuna Barnes

And my first question
will be, *Do you remember*
when we were both made
of bone—
I already can't bear
your reply
(What does it matter?)
There's barely a day I don't fear
the rain—
It matters because I'd like to know
whether I should expect
to make yet another
thing run off (a polished
finish will do that)
See, my fingers
slid off the ivory keys
once and for all, and then
my heart slipped out of my core
By luck, wisdom stayed—
Wisdom,
I always did like it
rough

SENTIENCE (CONT'D)

Just weeks to go
before the ground gives
its peppermint recitals again
& I'll go off
rocking
that lost look I have—
leaden beasts making a den
of the chest
(that's the best way
to put it)
Once, someone recommended
touch as cure:
then I felt hands
on my chest like hot stones
They didn't look
to feel, but pressed
hard & deep, until I felt
a slow current
pushing up
against the coast
What happened next was
the most extraordinary
thing
in that it was
completely
unexpected:
a dark flash & an endless string
of mornings

SWALLOWS

I've consoled myself into a knitted shape,
bending to the command of
slow rooms, lamplit
pinecones, the government
of phony twine & burlap
A little pomade, please
in my outstretched
hand—give me the blurred brush
of ambivalence,
opaqueness,
something less common
something like a ravine
a bed, a frontline
or the shrinking of optimism
in bad weather

VIGILANCE

The pale beating of morning
Small insomnias holding the bold larks in contempt
The day, its larceny
Of the sedated reeds always in a muddle
Their infested winding, their waists
Like glass
Leaning sweetly
Our long bodies are sleepy forests
Only the prowl of wrecked birds
Contracts our wingspan

THE THEN & NOW OF DUSKS

There is elegance in being
governed—shedding
the surplus,
tending only to matters
of pure existence
leaning back into
formless days & their obsidian
counterparts
like a hollow stalk
painted into the
blend—this beautiful
business of being
invisible,
deserted,
with only the primeval utility
of a claw
I can't remember
a single lead-in
for small talk
Won't you call a cab, please
This just
isn't working
out & I'm still afraid
of the night

THE LETTER

Even my sleeves hurt
this morning
I'm a newborn under lamplight
—a small regiment of ache
claiming its turf again
The wingspan of discord
really is
quite tremendous: as lasting
as the eyeless rain
(but all muscle)
What we find in each other
even sedated:
never a scaffold
never a suture
barely a place where the pulsing
can quiet
to a legible lament

SUBSTANCE

Take the lovers & their liquid
arms in their moonlight vestibules
Take the taciturn grasses
that the dogs look at
with sad eyes
Take the train stations
that multiply, the bridges
setting themselves aflame:
love still has become something
we do
like eating things
out of the fridge
to make room
I remember
our strange pilgrimages
into shadeless hearts
in pursuit of so much imaginary
tenderness—
Can you imagine
if someone had told us then
that really, love, and life, and it all
is just more
long & lonely mute
chrome

THE ONLY LOVE POEM

The rest is silence—I am not one
to reflect the sun,
you've reminded me once more,
and I wonder
what it must be
to always be
interested
in the opposite
of darkness—not merriment
or the sounding of
gongs so much
as the clean
footsteps
of foxes or the sober
repose
of stiff oaks
in outmoded
coats
I suppose I am bleak
It's all gray
shores and the next
war to me
Good thing you are
constantly coming in
like the weather,
uprooting
my frenzied reign—
how would we ever live
happily
without your
sagacity

NOTES

This Notes section is intended as part genealogy for the work, part ongoing reflection. Many of these poems use found language or a process. For instance, A MONTH OF GRIEVANCES repurposes language from famous World War I poems—by Siegfried Sassoon and Wilfred Owen, most significantly—in some cases through erasures, in others through reordering of certain key words, plays on words, and sampled phrases. I have endeavored to include as many references as I recall and the root of the impulse behind each poem.

What Was

ARGUMENT

A small white house, a laughing man and wife, / Deep snow. I turn it over in my palm / And watch it snowing in another life, / Another world, and from this scene learn what / It is to stand apart ("The Paperweight" by Gjertrud Schnackenberg)

JUNIPERS

'I feel there is an angel in me' she'd say / 'whom I am constantly shocking' (#8 from *Pictures of the Gone World* by Lawrence Ferlinghetti)
& my eyes caught a flood & I turned / looking for someone who would understand / I'd just seen my angel ("Central City Senior Center, New Orleans" by Aracelis Girmay)
I think / the angels must look something like this, / like somebody weeping ("The Angel (III)" by Franz Wright)

THE ROAD

There are no starfish in the sky tonight, / . . . / And there are cold evenings in your eyes. ("Amaranth" by Frank Stanford)
There never were stars / shaking on the surface or stars sinking. / The fish dream as the stars fall past them. ("Sea Levels" by Joanna Klink)

THE PEPPER SHAKERS WERE FILLED TO THE BRIM WITH HOSTS OF SWALLOWS

It was part of the colossal sun, / Surrounded by its choral rings, / Still far away. ("Not Ideas about the Thing but the Thing Itself" by Wallace Stevens)
She heard a gun go off and one hair turned gray. ("The Note" by Franz Wright)

This form draws from "Histoire d'un Amour (Cinéma)" by Jacques Roubaud and the first lines of "Petite Morale Elémentaire Portative" by Frédéric Forte (itself derived from Raymond Queneau's *morale élémentaire* form):

Mois pensif   Toit pentu / . . . / Pensée tue   Pensée tue / Toit

Both poems can be found in *Anthologie de l'OuLiPo* (Paris: Gallimard, 2009)

*

A Month of Grievances

One in five mothers develops birth-related post-traumatic stress disorder. As a recently postpartum mother, this statistic made me curious about the common wounds soldiers and mothers might share, their relative lack of agency in war and birth, and the climate of anxiety and tension surrounding them (the perceived or imposed sanctity of their respective roles). I wondered what would come from engaging with war poetry and ended up immersed in the work of Siegfried Sassoon, Wilfred Owen, Edward Thomas, and some. I became most engaged with Sassoon and Owen, mainly because of the combination of horror and beauty in these poems, and discovered an unexpected intersection of vernaculars from two worlds at opposite ends. What would come from portraying the strangely insular emotional environment of the mother through the familiar echoes of these old sufferers? Could the speakers, meandering through their respective fields, in the shocking aftermath of a great upheaval, meld somehow? Building gateways to Owen and Sassoon often came through the form of referential phrases.

In "Optimism," for instance, the reader will find the *ars poetica* behind this short series: "I tell you, in the voice / of the old poet: move it / into the sun," from Wilfred Owen's "Futility." The sun itself was of relevance to this process, as I was reading these war poems outdoors, squinting sometimes to make out the words (having sat on and destroyed my glasses again) and consequently misreading this or that word, misreadings that were incorporated. For example, Owen's famous "three parts shell" ("A Terre") became "three parts hell," and so on. "Repression of War Experience" by Sassoon was one of the touchstones through which this group of poems came to be, because of the "jabber" and the "trees." This brought Virginia Woolf's *Septimus* to mind, and then Woolf herself, leading me, through what one might call a sort of vernacular-based logic, to *The Waves*. Djuna Barnes followed with *Nightwood*, and thus resulted BLUR and MIGHT. The conception of these poems occurred through various processes, including but not limited to word mining, erasures, and collage. Additionally, a single resulting poem may have had multiple original war poems as sources (and vice versa). Lines that were particularly crucial to the resulting poem (whether serving as its impetus or appearing in some more or less distorted form) are listed below.

The volumes referenced in this project are *Collected Poems, 1908–1956* by Siegfried Sassoon (London: Faber and Faber, 1984) and *The Collected Poems of Wilfred Owen* (New York: New Directions, 1965). *Poems of the Great War, 1914–1918* (London: Penguin Books, 1998) was also referenced for word-mining purposes in the early stages. The authors' names are abbreviated below as W.O. and S.S. Works and names of other authors who influenced these poems are spelled out.

NEGOTIATION

From "Exposure" (W.O.):
. . . on us the doors are closed,— / We turn back to our dying.
All their eyes are ice, / But nothing happens.

EXPECTATIONS

Here is the real world / given in exchange for that illusion of weather you call *life* ("Thoughts on Fog," by Joanna Klink)
And the fact that we have to hurt ourselves / If it's all to go singingly. ("Time and Money" by Andrzej Sosnowski)

AFTERNOON

Partial erasure of "Attack" (S.S.):
   At dawn the ridge emerges massed and dun / In the wild purple of the glow'ring
   sun

DISAGREEMENT

Reorganizes lexicon from "Thrushes" (S.S.):
   Tossed on the glittering air they soar and skim, / Whose voices make the
   emptiness of light / a windy palace.
   Who hears the cry of God in everything, / And storms the gate of nothingness
   for proof.

CONCERNS

And now the heavens are piled with darkening trouble ("Solar Eclipse," S.S.)
A lover with disaster in his face, / And scarlet blossom twisted in bright hair. /
'Afraid to fight . . . ' ("Ancient History," S.S.)

DISPATCH

Erasure of "Repression of War Experience" (S.S.):
   . . . it's bad to think of war
   And it's been proved that soldiers don't go mad / Unless they lose control of ugly
   thoughts / That drive them out to jabber among the trees.

. . . roses hang their dripping heads. / Books; . . . / Standing so quiet and patient
on their shelves
You sit and gnaw your nails, and let your pipe out
There's one big, dizzy moth that bumps and flutters

THE UNMENTIONABLE WORSHIP OF IDLE AFTERNOONS

From "On Scratchbury Camp" (S.S.):
Along the grave green downs, this idle afternoon, / Shadows . . . bring, like
unfoldment of a flower, the best of June. / Shadows outspread in spacious
movement . . .
. . . larks, ascending shrill, praised freedom as they flew.
Cloud shadows drifting slow . . . / . . . / I watch them go.
. . . the skies were still; / Larks were singing ("Stand-to: Good Friday Morning," S.S.)
From "Glory of Women" (S.S.):
When hell's last horror breaks them, and they run, / Trampling the terrible
corpses—blind with blood. / O German mother dreaming by the fire, / While
you are knitting socks to send your son / His face is trodden deeper in the mud.
There's no end to this. ("The Dream" by Marie Howe)

RESOLUTION

I can rebuild you in my brain, / Through you've gone out patrolling in the dark.
("To Any Dead Officer," S.S.)
'Soon I'll be in open fields,' he thought, / And half remembered starlight on the
meadows, / Scent of mown grass and voices of tired men ("Haunted," S.S.)
Night. He was blind; he could not see the stars ("The Death Bed," S.S.)
Their faces are the fair, unshrouded night, / And planets are their eyes, their ageless
dreams. ("The Dragon and the Undying," S.S.)

OPPOSITION

There, with much work to do before the light, / We lugged our clay-sucked boots as
best we might / Along the trench ("The Redeemer," S.S.)

DEVOTION

Safe quit of wars, I speed you on your way / Up lonely, glimmering fields to find
new day, / Slow-rising, saintless, confident and kind ("To His Dead Body," S.S.)
. . . then the gloom / Swallowed his sense of sight; he stooped and swore / Because
a sagging wire had caught his neck. ("A Working Party," S.S.)
(You know how bees come into a twilight room / From dazzling afternoon, then
sail away / Out of the curtained gloom.) ("To a Very Wise Man," S.S.)

OPTIMISM

Reorganizes lexicon from "Futility" (W.O.):
    Move him into the sun—

REVELATION

It seemed that out of battle I escaped / Down some profound dull tunnel, long since scooped / Through granites which titanic wars had groined. ("Strange Meeting," W.O.)

NONCHALANCE

To miss the march of this retreating world / Into vain citadels that are not walled. ("Strange Meeting," W.O.)
O starshine on the fields of long-ago, / Bring me the darkness and the nightingale ("Memory," S.S.)
I have observed her evening-party eyes ("Breach of Decorum," S.S.)

APOLOGY

His face is trodden deeper in the mud. ("Glory of Women," S.S.)

POLITICS

From "How to Die" (S.S.):
    Radiance reflected in his eyes, / And on his lips a whispered name. / You'd
    think, to hear some people talk, / That lads go West with sobs and curses, /
    . . . / Hankering for wreaths and tombs and hearses.

OPINIONS

Observe these blue solemnities of sky ("Solar Eclipse," S.S.)

PERSISTENCE

The bronzed battalions of the stricken wood / In whose lament I hear a voice that grieves ("Autumn," S.S.)

INTIMATE

. . . muttering creatures underground / Who hear the boom of shells in muffled sound. ("The Rear Guard," S.S.)
& all day long, people going in & out / of each other, their houses, the supermarket. ("They Tell Me You Are Gone" by Aracelis Girmay)
Voices moving about in the quiet house: / Thud of feet and a muffled shutting of doors: / Everyone yawning. ("Falling Asleep," S.S.)

Marveling that any came alive / Out of the shambles that men built ("Song-Books of the War," S.S.)

COUPLES GOING NUDE INTO THE SAD WATER

And in the poet's plangent dream I saw / no Lorelei upon the Rhone / nor angels debarked at Marseilles / but couples going nude into the sad water ("4" from *Pictures of the Gone World* by Lawrence Ferlinghetti)

From "Song-Books of the War" (S.S.):

> In fifty years, when peace outshines / Remembrance of the battle lines
> And then he'll speak of Haig's last drive, / Marveling that any came alive / Out
> of the shambles that men built / And smashed, to cleanse the world of guilt.

WONDERMENT

. . . But many there stood still / To face the stark, blank sky beyond the ridge, / Knowing their feet had come to the end of the world. / Marveling they stood ("Spring Offensive," W.O.)

LITTORAL

. . . Through the park / Voices of boys rang saddening like a hymn, / . . . / Till gathering sleep had mothered them from him. ("Disabled," W.O.)

ACRIMONY

The dying soldier shifts his head / To watch the glory that returns; / He lifts his fingers toward the skies / Where holy brightness breaks in flame ("How to Die," S.S.)

ALL THE ARTS OF HURTING

Erasure and collage from "A Terre" (W.O.):

> Sit on the bed. I'm blind, and three parts shell.
> . . . I'd willingly be puffy, bald, / And patriotic. Buffers catch from boys /
> At least the jokes hurled at them. I suppose / Little I'd ever teach a son, but
> hitting, / Shooting, war, hunting, all the arts of hurting.
> . . . Microbes have their joys

I must be crazy; I learn from the daisy. ("The Calls," W.O.)

PROPOSAL

Down the close, darkening lanes ("The Send-Off," W.O.)

THE IMMORTELLES OF PERFECT PITCH

There are the mud-flowers of dialect / And the immortelles of perfect pitch ("Song" by Seamus Heaney)

Reorganizes lexicon from "All Sounds Have Been as Music" (W.O.)
Down the glimmering staircase, past the pensive clock, / Childhood creeps on tiptoe, fumbles at the lock. (#8 from "Vigils," S.S.)

SEDUCTION ACT

. . . Yet search till gray sea heaves, / And I will wind among these fields for him. / Gaze, daisy! / Stare through haze and glare ("Elegy in April and September (*jabbered among the trees*)," W.O.)

PARAMETERS

Now earth has stopped their piteous mouths that coughed. ("Greater Love," W.O.)

MERCY

This book is not about heroes . . . nor is it about . . . dominion. . . . Yet these elegies are to this generation in no sense consolatory. (From the preface to *The Collected Poems of Wilfred Owen*, New Directions)

BEGINNINGS

"Pushing up daisies" is their creed, you know. / To grain, then, go my fat, to buds my sap, / For all the usefulness there is in soap. ("A Terre," W.O.)

SATURNINE

Dullness best solves / The tease and doubt of shelling ("Insensibility," W.O.)

*

Blur / Might

Lexicon for the poems in these two sections was drawn in large part from *The Waves* by Virginia Woolf (New York: Harvest Books, 1978) and *Nightwood* by Djuna Barnes (London: Faber and Faber, 2015) and continues to draw from Sassoon and Owen. Word mining across the entire books (as opposed to individual poems) was used as primary process.

WHAT WAS SAID

Persistent echoing / in all sound that means good-bye, good-bye— ("End of Winter" by Louise Glück)

THE QUESTION OF SURRENDER

Primeval days were dull. Events existed / As unexploited masses of material.

("Lines Written in Anticipation of a London Paper Attaining a Guaranteed
Circulation of Ten Million Daily," S.S.)

AN AUTOBIOGRAPHY OF ASPHALT

Monday came down soft and sad / Like a gray sky and broke. ("No Eliot for You
Today" by Kevin Tsai)

WINDING DOWN

And the night smells like snow. ("Night Walk" by Franz Wright)
You will imagine our face as the fire overtook us / sliding under our feet at a little
past noon ("Pompeii, **A.D.** 79" by Emily Fragos)

ONE DOG WILL FIND US BOTH

Variation on "Nora will leave that girl some day; but though those two are buried at
the opposite ends of the earth, one dog will find them both." (*Nightwood* by Djuna
Barnes)

THE THEN & NOW OF DUSKS

This isn't working out, is it ("The Street" by Franz Wright)

For all the works I have unintentionally referenced or that have influenced me in
ways unknown, thank you and sincere apologies.

ACKNOWLEDGMENTS

Grateful acknowledgment is made to the editors of the following journals in which these poems first appeared, sometimes under different titles and in other forms: "Argument" in *Phantom* (Kelly Forsythe, Ryann Stevenson, and Brian Russell); "The Pepper Shakers Were Filled to the Brim with Hosts of Swallows" and "Death Toll" in *Blunderbuss Magazine* (Sam Ross); "A Month of Grievances" (entire section) in *VERSE* (Brian Henry and Andrew Zawacki); "What Was Said" and "Tête-à-Tête" in *The Offing* (Mahogany L. Browne, Connie Ni Chiu, and Jayy Dodd); "One Dog Will Find Us Both" and "Winding Down" in *Two Peach* (Catherine Pond and Julia Anna Morrison).

Many thanks to Jon Tribble and the team and staff at the Crab Orchard Series in Poetry and Southern Illinois University Press. Sincere thanks to Chad Davidson for seeing a light in this book.

Thank you to my teachers, whether alive or winged, who patiently endured this or any previous work: Lucie Brock-Broido, Emily Fragos, Sophie Cabot Black, Eamon Grennan, and Richard Howard. Thank you, Nicholas Christopher, for Mosaics, and thank you, Mónica de la Torre, for Traditions of Rupture, two of the most beautifully crafted classes I've been given to take. Thank you, Sylvère Lotringer, for your teachings and support. Deepest gratitude goes out especially to Idra Novey, who gives *endlessly* and thus sustains.

Thank you to the various communities and individuals whose heart and acumen have maintained me in unnamable and crucial ways, including first beloved contact Diana Khoi Nguyen and companions Jay Deshpande, Marina Blitshteyn, Elizabeth Clark Wessel, Iris Cushing, Julia Guez, Sam Ross, and Joshua Daniel Edwin. For their comments along the way, thank you (alphabetically) to Kirkwood Adams, Lauren Birden, Sharif El Gammal-Ortiz, Sasha Fletcher, John James, Kate Jenkins, Sarah Johnson, Julie Kantor, Kat Laskowski, Keegan Lester, JC Longbottom, Montana Ray, Eva Maria Saavedra, and Alison Sweet. To any former classmates or colleagues who shared their hearts and did me the honor of applying their consideration to my work: thank you. Thank you also to Yardenne Greenspan, Tony Mancus, Tanya Paperny, and David Varno. Thank you to Bianca Spriggs, Safiya Sinclair, Malachi Black, and the late Franz Wright for allowing me to sit with your beautiful and urgent work. And to Katerina Stoykova-Klemer, thank you.

To the Paul & Daisy Soros Fellowship for New Americans, especially the class of 2010, thank you for the love, always. Special thanks to Sina Kian and Yifan Xu.

Other individuals whose tender souls have sat by mine and whom I wish to thank include Megan Hatch, Stephanie Christopher, Melissa Yap-Stewart, Robert

Stewart, and Karlie Parry. Thank you to Annalise, Catherine, Kate, Jessie, Linda, Katherine, and Beth. And deepest thanks to the ever-loved Anna-Katharina Späni, Mélanie Goldschmid, and Kilandamoko Vuandaba. Thank you, finally and especially, to Scott Martin, Barbara Belli-Poole, Dominique Belli, Clara Martin, Catherine Poole, Elizabeth Bennett, Christiane Schenk, and my sister, Jenn. I love you; that is all.

Thank you, P.P., for throwing me in. Hope the wings fit.

To my children: my loves, my safe place, the source of all awe.

OTHER BOOKS IN THE CRAB ORCHARD SERIES IN POETRY

Muse
Susan Aizenberg

Millennial Teeth
Dan Albergotti

Hijra
Hala Alyan

Instructions, Abject & Fuming
Julianna Baggott

Lizzie Borden in Love:
Poems in Women's Voices
Julianna Baggott

This Country of Mothers
Julianna Baggott

The Black Ocean
Brian Barker

Vanishing Acts
Brian Barker

Nostalgia for a World
Where We Can Live
Monica Berlin

The Sphere of Birds
Ciaran Berry

White Summer
Joelle Biele

Gold Bee
Bruce Bond

Rookery
Traci Brimhall

USA-1000
Sass Brown

The Gospel according to Wild Indigo
Cyrus Cassells

In Search of the Great Dead
Richard Cecil

Twenty First Century Blues
Richard Cecil

Circle
Victoria Chang

Errata
Lisa Fay Coutley

Salt Moon
Noel Crook

Consolation Miracle
Chad Davidson

From the Fire Hills
Chad Davidson

The Last Predicta
Chad Davidson

Furious Lullaby
Oliver de la Paz

Names above Houses
Oliver de la Paz

Dots & Dashes
Jehanne Dubrow

The Star-Spangled Banner
Denise Duhamel

Smith Blue
Camille T. Dungy

Seam
Tarfia Faizullah

Beautiful Trouble
Amy Fleury

Sympathetic Magic
Amy Fleury

Egg Island Almanac
Brendan Galvin

Soluble Fish
Mary Jo Firth Gillett

Pelican Tracks
Elton Glaser

Winter Amnesties
Elton Glaser

Strange Land
Todd Hearon

View from True North
Sara Henning

Always Danger
David Hernandez

Heavenly Bodies
Cynthia Huntington

Terra Nova
Cynthia Huntington

Zion
TJ Jarrett

Red Clay Suite
Honorée Fanonne Jeffers

Fabulae
Joy Katz

Cinema Muto
Jesse Lee Kercheval

Train to Agra
Vandana Khanna

The Primitive Observatory
Gregory Kimbrell

If No Moon
Moira Linehan

Incarnate Grace
Moira Linehan

For Dust Thou Art
Timothy Liu

Strange Valentine
A. Loudermilk

Dark Alphabet
Jennifer Maier

Lacemakers
Claire McQuerry

Tongue Lyre
Tyler Mills

Oblivio Gate
Sean Nevin

Holding Everything Down
William Notter

American Flamingo
Greg Pape

Crossroads and Unholy Water
Marilene Phipps

Birthmark
Jon Pineda

No Acute Distress
Jennifer Richter

Threshold
Jennifer Richter

On the Cusp of a Dangerous Year
Lee Ann Roripaugh

Year of the Snake
Lee Ann Roripaugh

Misery Prefigured
J. Allyn Rosser

*Into Each Room We Enter
without Knowing*
Charif Shanahan

In the Absence of Clocks
Jacob Shores-Arguello

Glaciology
Jeffrey Skinner

Roam
Susan B. A. Somers-Willett

The Laughter of Adam and Eve
Jason Sommer

*Huang Po and the
Dimensions of Love*
Wally Swist

Persephone in America
Alison Townsend

Spitting Image
Kara van de Graaf

Becoming Ebony
Patricia Jabbeh Wesley

Abide
Jake Adam York

A Murmuration of Starlings
Jake Adam York

Persons Unknown
Jake Adam York